Weekend Knits

Volume 2

Easy To Knit

Kitchen Towels and Dish Cloths

Copyright © 2014 Vicki Becker.
All rights reserved worldwide.

Copyright Information Page

Copyright © 2014 Vicki Becker.

All rights reserved worldwide.

No part of this publication may be replicated, redistributed, or given away in any form or by any means, including scanning, photocopying, or otherwise without the prior written consent of the copyright holder.

You have permission to sell items you personally make from the patterns but not for commercial or mass production purposes. You do not, however, have permission to use my photographs to sell your items.

All patterns are sold in good faith. Every effort has been made to ensure that all instructions are accurate and complete.

Vicki Becker

www.vickisdesigns.com

First Printing, 2014
ISBN-13: 978-1500666125
ISBN-10: 1500666122

Printed in the United States of America

Contents

Copyright Information Page 2
Introduction 5
Skill Level Definitions 7
General Instructions 9
Common Knitting Phrases 11
Abbreviations 13
Knitting Terms 15
Knitting Needle Conversion 16
Denim Blues Hanging Towel 17
Denim Blues Dishcloth 21
Violets Hanging Towel 23
Violets Dishcloth 27
I'll Wash You Dry Hanging Towel 29
I'll Wash You Dry Dishcloth 33
Lavender Fields Hanging Towel 35
Lavender Fields Dishcloth 39
Red Raspberries Hanging Towel 41
Red Raspberries Dishcloth 45
Sunshine Hanging Towel 47
Sunshine Dishcloth 51
Helpful Hints 53
Conclusion 57

Introduction

Why knit a dishcloth? First dishcloths are excellent projects for beginners. They are also great projects for more experienced knitters who want to make a quick gift or want a project they can complete start to finish in a day.

These hanging kitchen towels and dishcloths are quick and easy to make. You can knit a set in just a weekend using cotton yarns and number 9 knitting needles. They are knitted using interesting textured patterns that may look complicated but are actually very easy to knit. Kitchen towel sets make great gifts or a nice addition to your own kitchen!

The skill levels for the patterns are beginner and easy. You should, however, already know the basic stitches and how to read patterns. You need to know how to cast on, knit, purl, yarn over, knit two together, and bind off.

Included in this book are pattern instructions for 6 different kitchen towels with matching dishcloths. At the end of the book in the helpful hint section there are detailed instructions for blocking your dishcloths.

I hope you enjoy making these easy to knit kitchen towel sets.

Skill Level Definitions

Beginner
A beginner project is for first-time knitters using basic knit and purl stitches. Beginner projects have minimal shaping.

Easy
Projects using basic stitches, repetitive stitch patterns, simple color changes, and simple shaping and finishing.

Intermediate
Intermediate projects have a variety of stitches, such as basic cables and lace, simple intarsia, double-pointed needles and knitting in the round needle techniques. This level has mid-level shaping and finishing.

Experienced
Projects using advanced techniques and stitches, such as short rows, fair isle, more intricate intarsia, cables, lace patterns, and numerous color changes.

General Instructions

Gauge

Gauge is determined by the tightness or looseness of your work and will affect the finished size of your project. Needle sizes given in instructions are only guides and should never be used without first making a sample swatch.

Understanding Symbols

A single asterisk (*) mean to repeat the instructions following the asterisk as directed. For example, *K1, P1. Rep from * to end of row.

Two asterisks (* *) mean to repeat the instructions between the two asterisks as directed.

Parenthesis is used to set off a group of instructions worked in the place directed. For example, "(K1, P1) in next st".

Brackets [ ] mean to work instructions between the brackets as many times as directed. For example, [K1, P1] 5 times.

How to read patterns with multiple sizes

When knitting a pattern with multiple sizes parentheses are used to include additional information for other sizes. Directions are given for the smallest size, with the larger sizes in parentheses. For example, if the instructions read cast on 12 (14, 16), you would cast on 12 for size small, 14 for medium, and 16 for large.

Standard Yarn Weight System

Most yarn and thread now come with a weight number on the wrapper. I provide the weight number of the yarn or thread I used to design each pattern. This makes it much easier to make substitutions.

Common Knitting Phrases

Some instruction phrases used in knitting patterns can be confusing. Here are some common knitting phrases and their meanings.

as established: To repeat a series of steps or patterns.

back of your work: The side of your work that faces away from you when holding your needles.

front of your work: The side of your work that faces you when holding your needles.

The preceding two terms are referring to the side of your work that is currently facing you or faces away from you and not the wrong side (WS) or right side (RS) of the article you are knitting.

bind off: Used to finish an edge or segment. Lift the first stitch over the second, the second over the third, etc.

bind off in ribbing: Work in ribbing as you bind off. Knit the knit stitches, purl the purl stitches.

cast on: Placing a foundation row of stitches on the needle in order to begin knitting.

decrease: Reduce the stitches in a row by knitting or purling 2 together.

end with a WS row: Finish the section you're working on by working a wrong side row last.

end with a RS row: Finish the section you're working on by working a right side row last.

Garter Stitch: Knit every row.

knitwise: Insert the right needle into the stitch as if you were going to knit it.

make one: Make a new stitch by lifting the yarn in the space between the stitches. With the needle tip, lift the strand between the last stitch knit and the next stitch on the left hand needle and knit into the back of it. One knit stitch has been added.

make one p-st: Make a new stitch by lifting the yarn in the space between the stitches. With the needle tip, lift the strand between the last stitch worked and the next stitch on the left hand needle and purl it. One purl stitch has been added.

pick up and knit (purl): Use a separate strand of yarn to create a row of stitches on a needle by pulling loops through along a knitted edge.

pm (place marker): Place a loop of contrasting yarn or purchased stitch marker between stitches on your needle to indicate the beginning of a round as in circular knitting or to mark a specific pattern repeat.

purlwise: Insert the right needle into the stitch as if you were going to purl it.

slip stitch (sl st): An un-worked stitch made by passing a stitch from the left hand to the right hand needle.

Stockinette Stitch: Knit right side rows and purl wrong side rows.

Circular knitting: Knit all rounds.

Reverse Stockinette Stitch: The purl side of stockinette stitch. Purled on the right side of the work and knitted on the wrong side.

work even: Continue in whatever stitch pattern you're using without increasing or decreasing.

work to end: Work in whatever stitch pattern you're using to the end of the row.

yarn over (yo): Making a new stitch by wrapping the yarn over the right hand needle.

Abbreviations

Knitting Abbreviations

beg	beginning	patt (s)	pattern (s)
bet	between	pm	place marker
BO	bind off	psso	pass slipped st over
CC	contrasting color	pwise	purl wise
cn	cable needle	RH	right hand
CO	cast on	rem	remaining
dec	decrease	rep	repeat
dpn	double pointed needles	rnd (s)	round (s)
inc	increase	RS	right side
k	knit	sk	skip

k tbl	knit stitch through the back loops	sl	slip a stitch
kwise	knit wise	sp	space
kf&b	knit in the front and back of same stitch	st (s)	stitch (es)
k2tog	knit 2 together	St st	stockinette stitch
LH	left hand	tbl	through back loop
lp (s)	loop (s)	tog	together
M1	make 1 (an increase)	WS	wrong side
MC	main color	wyib	with yarn in back
p	purl	wyif	with yarn in front
p tbl	purl through the back loops	y fwd	yarn forward
p2tog	purl 2 together	yon/yo	yarn over needle yarn over
pfb	purl in the front and back of same stitch	yrn	yarn round needle

British vs American Knitting Terms

British English	US-American English
Tension	Gauge
Stocking Stitch	Stockinette Stitch
Grafting	Kitchener Stitch
Moss Stitch	Seed Stitch
Yarn Forward	Yarn Over
Cast Off	Bind Off

** All pattern instructions use US terms. **

Knitting Needle Conversion

Knitting Needle Sizes

US	UK	Metric
4		3.5mm
5	9	3.7mm
6	8	4.0mm
7	7	4.5mm
8	6	5.0mm
9	5	5.5mm
10	4	6.0mm
10 1/2	3	6.5mm
11	0	8.0mm
13	00	9.0mm
15	000	10.0mm
17		12.0mm
19		16.0mm
35		19.0mm
50		25.0mm

** All pattern instructions use US terms. **

Denim Blues Hanging Towel

Instructions

Skill Level: Easy

Size: 13 1/2 X 13 1/2 inches

Materials: Lily Sugar'N Cream Cotton Yarn, or and #4 Medium weight cotton yarn.

2.5 oz (70.9g) Approximately 120 yards

Tapestry or yarn needle

Sewing needle and matching thread

1- 1 inch button

Needles: Size 9 (5.5mm) or size to obtain gauge.

Gauge: 4 sts and 6 rows = 1 inch

Cast on 54 sts.

Row 1: (RS) *K1, P1, K3, P1, rep from * to end of row.

Row 2: (WS) Repeat row 1.

Row 3: (RS) P across row.

Row 4: (WS) *K1, P 5, rep from * to end of row.

Repeat these 4 rows for pattern. Work until towel is 10 inches in length ending with a WS row.

Pattern Detail

Top Shaping

Row 1: (RS) *K1, K2tog, rep from * to end of row. 36 sts.

Row 2: (WS) *K1, K2tog, rep from * to end of row. 24 sts.

Row 3: (RS) *K2tog across row. 12 sts.

Row 4-5: K across row.

Row 6: (WS) *K1, K2tog, rep from * to end of row. 8 sts.

Hanging Tab

Continue knitting each row on 8 sts until hanging tab measures 5 1/2 inches.

Buttonhole

Row 1: K2, K2tog, Yo twice, K2tog, K2.

Row 2: K3, K1 in first Yo, P1 in second Yo, K3.

Row 3-5: K across row.

Row 6: K2tog, K4, K2tog.

Row 7: Bind off.

Buttonhole Detail

Finishing

With tapestry needle, weave in ends. Sew button to the right side of the hanging towel as shown in photo. Block if desired.

Denim Blues Dishcloth

Instructions

Skill Level: Beginner

Size: 10 1/2 inches square

Materials: Lily Sugar'N Cream Cotton Yarn, or #4 Medium weight cotton yarn.

2 oz (56.7g) Approximately 95 yards

Tapestry or yarn needle

Needles: Size 9 (5.5mm) or size to obtain gauge.

Gauge: 4 sts and 6 rows = 1 inch

Cast on 42 sts.

Border

Rows 1-3: K each st across.

Pattern Rows

Row 1: (RS) K3, *K1, P1, K3, P1, rep from * to last 3 sts, K3.

Row 2: (WS) Repeat row 1.

Row 3: (RS) K3, P across row to last 3 sts, K3.

Row 4: (WS) K3, *K1, P5, rep from * to last 3 sts, K3.

Repeat rows 1-4 for pattern.

Repeat pattern rows until cloth is 10 inches long. Rep rows 1-3 of border. Bind off.

Finishing

With tapestry or yarn needle weave in ends. Block if desired.

Pattern Detail

Violets Hanging Towel

Instructions

Skill Level: Easy

Size: 13 1/2 X 13 1/2 inches

Materials: Lily Sugar'N Cream Cotton Yarn, or #4 Medium weight cotton yarn.

2.5 oz (70.9g) Approximately 120 yards

Tapestry or yarn needle

Sewing needle and matching thread

1- 1 inch button

Needles: Size 9 (5.5mm) or size to obtain gauge.

Gauge: 4 sts and 6 rows = 1 inch

Cast on 54 sts.

Row 1: (RS) *K5, P1, rep from *, ending with P1.

Row 2: (WS) Sl 1, K1, *P3, K3, rep from * ending with K1.

Row 3: (RS) Sl 1, P1, *K1, P5, rep from *, ending with P3.

Row 4: (WS) Sl 1, P2, *K1, P5, repeat from *, ending with P2.

Row 5: (RS) Sl 1, *P3, K3, rep from *, ending with K2.

Row 6: (WS) Sl 1, K4, P1, *K5, P1, rep from * to end of row.

Repeat these 6 rows for pattern. Work until towel is 10 inches in length ending with a WS row.

Stitch Detail

Top Shaping

Row 1: (RS) *K1, K2tog, rep from * to end of row. 36 sts.

Row 2: (WS) *K1, K2tog, rep from * to end of row. 24 sts.

Row 3: (RS) *K2tog across row. 12 sts.

Row 4-5: K across row.

Row 6: (WS) *K1, K2tog, rep from * to end of row. 8 sts.

Hanging Tab

Continue knitting each row on 8 sts until hanging tab measures 5 1/2 inches.

Buttonhole

Row 1: K2, K2tog, Yo twice, K2tog, K2.

Row 2: K3, K1 in first Yo, P1 in second Yo, K3.

Row 3-5: K across row.

Row 6: K2tog, K4, K2tog.

Row 7: Bind off.

Buttonhole detail

Finishing

With tapestry needle, weave in ends. Sew button to the right side of the hanging towel as shown in photo. Block if desired.

Violets Dishcloth

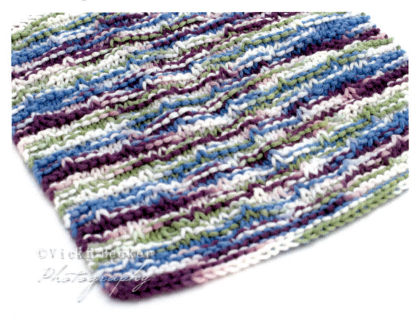

Instructions

Skill Level: Beginner

Size: 10 1/2 inches square

Materials: Lily Sugar'N Cream Cotton Yarn, or #4 Medium weight cotton yarn.

2 oz (56.7g) Approximately 95 yards

Tapestry or yarn needle

Needles: Size 9 (5.5mm) or size to obtain gauge.

Gauge: 4 sts and 6 rows = 1 inch

Cast on 42 sts.

Border

Rows 1-6: K each st across.

Pattern Rows

Row 1: (RS) K3, *K5, P1, rep from * to last 3 sts, K3.

Row 2: (WS) K5, *P3, K3, rep from * to last 4 sts, K4.

Row 3: (RS) K4, P1, *K1, P5, rep from * to last 7 sts, K1, P3, K3.

Row 4: (WS) K4, P2, *K1, P5, rep from * to last 6 sts, K1, P2, K3.

Row 5: (RS) K4, *P3, K3, rep from * to last 5 sts, K5.

Row 6: (WS) K3, *K5, P1, rep from * to last 3 sts, K3.

Repeat rows 1-6 for pattern.

Repeat pattern rows until cloth is 9 1/2 inches long. Rep rows 1-6 of border and bind off.

Finishing

With tapestry or yarn needle weave in ends. Block if desired.

I'll Wash You Dry Hanging Towel

Instructions

Skill Level: Easy

Size: 13 1/2 X 13 1/2 inches

Materials: Lily Sugar'N Cream Cotton Yarn, or #4 Medium weight cotton yarn.

2.5 oz (70.9g) Approximately 120 yards

Tapestry or yarn needle

Sewing needle and matching thread

1- 1 inch button

Needles: Size 9 (5.5mm) or size to obtain gauge.

Spare Needle: Size 9 double pointed needle or cable needle.

Gauge: 4 sts and 6 rows = 1 inch

Cast on 54 sts.

Pattern Rows

Row 1: K

Row 2: *K2, P2. Repeat from * ending row with K2.

Row 3: *P2, slip 1 st on spare needle, K the next st, K the st from the spare needle. Repeat from * ending row with P2.

Row 4: P.

Row 5: K.

Row 6: *P2, K2. Repeat from * ending row with P2.

Row 7: *Slip 1 st on spare needle, K the next st, K the st from the spare needle, P2. Repeat from * ending row slip st on spare needle, K the next st, K the st from the spare needle.

Row 8: P.

Repeat these 8 rows for pattern. Work until towel is 10 inches in length.

Pattern Detail

Top Shaping

Row 1: *K1, K2tog, rep from * to end of row. 36 sts.

Row 2: *K1, K2tog, rep from * to end of row. 24 sts.

Row 3: *K2tog across row. 12 sts.

Row 4-5: K across row.

Row 6: *K1, K2tog, rep from * to end of row. 8 sts.

Hanging Tab

Continue knitting each row on 8 sts until hanging tab measures 5 1/2 inches.

Buttonhole

Row 1: K2, K2tog, Yo twice, K2tog, K2.

Row 2: K3, K1 in first Yo, P1 in second Yo, K3.

Row 3-5: K across row.

Row 6: K2tog, K4, K2tog.

Row 7: Bind off.

Buttonhole Detail

Finishing

With tapestry needle, weave in ends. Sew button to the right side of the hanging towel as shown in photo. Block if desired.

I'll Wash You Dry Dishcloth

Instructions

Skill Level: Easy

Size: 10 1/2 inches square

Materials: Lily Sugar'N Cream Cotton Yarn, or #4 Medium weight cotton yarn.

2 oz (56.7g) Approximately 95 yards

Tapestry or yarn needle

Needles: Size 9 (5.5mm) or size to obtain gauge.

Gauge: 4 sts and 6 rows = 1 inch

Cast on 42 sts.

Border

Rows 1-5: K each st across.

Pattern Rows

Row 1: K

Row 2: K4, *K2, P2. Repeat from * ending row with K2, K4.

Row 3: K4, *P2, slip 1 st on spare needle, K the next st, K the st from the spare needle. Repeat from * ending row P2, K4.

Row 4: P.

Row 5: K.

Row 6: K4, *P2, K2. Repeat from * ending row P2, K4.

Row 7: K4, *slip 1 st on spare needle, K the next st, K the st from the spare needle, P2. Repeat from * to the last 6 sts. Slip st on spare needle, K the next st, K the st from the spare needle, K4.

Row 8: P.

Repeat rows 1-8 for pattern.

Repeat pattern rows until cloth is 9 1/2 inches long. Rep rows 1-5 of border and bind off.

Finishing

With tapestry or yarn needle weave in ends. Block if desired.

Lavender Fields Hanging Towel

Instructions

Skill Level: Easy

Size: 14 1/2 X 13 1/2 inches

Materials: Lily Sugar'N Cream Cotton Yarn, or and #4 Medium weight cotton yarn.

2.5 oz (70.9g) Approximately 120 yards

Tapestry or yarn needle

Sewing needle and matching thread

1- 1 inch button

Needles: Size 9 (5.5mm) or size to obtain gauge.

Gauge: 4 sts and 6 rows = 1 inch

Cast on 58 sts.

Pattern Rows

Row 1: K

Row 2: K

Row 3: *K4, Yo, K2tog, K1, Yo, K2tog, rep from * ending with K4.

Row 4: Sl 1, P4, *K1, P2, K1, P5, rep from * ending with P4.

Repeat these 4 rows for pattern. Work until towel is 10 inches in length.

Pattern Detail

Top Shaping

Row 1: *K1, K2tog, rep from * to end of row. 39 sts.

Row 2: *K1, K2tog, rep from * to end of row. 26 sts.

Row 3: *K2, K2tog rep from * to end of row. 20 sts.

Row 4: K across row.

Row 5: K2tog across row. 10sts.

Row 6: K2, K2tog, K2, K2tog, K2. 8 sts.

Hanging Tab

Continue knitting each row on 8 sts until hanging tab measures 5 1/2 inches.

Buttonhole

Row 1: K2, K2tog, Yo twice, K2tog, K2.

Row 2: K3, K1 in first Yo, P1 in second Yo, K3.

Row 3-5: K across row.

Row 6: K2tog, K4, K2tog.

Row 7: Bind off.

Buttonhole Detail

Finishing

With tapestry needle, weave in ends. Sew button to the right side of the hanging towel as shown in photo. Block if desired.

Lavender Fields Dishcloth

Instructions

Skill Level: Beginner

Size: 9 3/4 inches square

Materials: Lily Sugar'N Cream Cotton Yarn, or #4 Medium weight cotton yarn.

2 oz (56.7g) Approximately 95 yards

Tapestry or yarn needle

Needles: Size 9 (5.5mm) or size to obtain gauge.

Gauge: 4 sts and 6 rows = 1 inch

Cast on 39 sts.

Border

Rows 1-4: K each st across.

Pattern Rows

Row 1: K.

Row 2: K.

Row 3: K4, *K4, Yo, K2tog, K1, Yo, K2tog, rep from * across row to last 8 sts, K8.

Row 4: K4, P5, *K1, P2, K1, P5, rep from * across row to last 8 sts, P4, K4.

Rep rows 1-4 for pattern.

Repeat pattern rows until cloth is 9 inches long ending with Row 2. Rep rows 1-4 of border. Bind off.

Finishing

With tapestry or yarn needle weave in ends. Block if desired.

Red Raspberries Hanging Towel

Instructions

Skill Level: Easy

Size: 13 1/2 X 13 1/2 inches

Materials: Lily Sugar'N Cream Cotton Yarn, or and #4 Medium weight cotton yarn.

2.5 oz (70.9g) Approximately 120 yards

Tapestry or yarn needle

Sewing needle and matching thread

1- 1 inch button

Needles: Size 9 (5.5mm) or size to obtain gauge.

Gauge: 4 sts and 6 rows = 1 inch

Cast on 53 sts.

Pattern

Row 1: K.

Row 2: Sl the first st. P across row.

Row 3: Sl the first st then K2tog across row.

Row 4: Sl the first st. *Make one, K1 rep from * across row.

Repeat rows 1-4 for pattern.

> Make One: Make a new stitch by lifting the yarn in the space between the stitches. With the needle tip, lift the strand between the last stitch knit and the next stitch on the left hand needle and knit into the back of it. One knit stitch has been added.

Pattern Detail

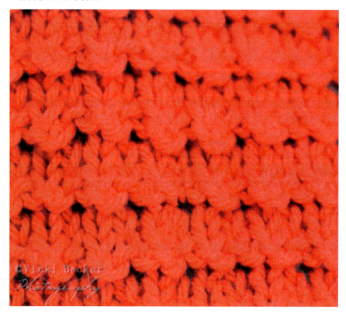

Top Shaping

Row 1: (RS) *K1, K2tog, rep from * ending row with K2tog, K2. 36 sts.

Row 2: (WS) *K1, K2tog, rep from * to end of row. 24 sts.

Row 3: (RS) *K2tog across row. 12 sts.

Row 4-5: K across row.

Row 6: (WS) *K1, K2tog, rep from * to end of row. 8 sts.

Hanging Tab

Continue knitting each row on 8 sts until hanging tab measures 5 1/2 inches.

Buttonhole

Row 1: K2, K2tog, Yo twice, K2tog, K2.

Row 2: K3, K1 in first Yo, P1 in second Yo, K3.

Row 3-5: K across row.

Row 6: K2tog, K4, K2tog.

Row 7: Bind off.

Buttonhole Detail

Finishing

With tapestry needle, weave in ends. Sew button to the right side of the hanging towel as shown in photo.

Red Raspberries Dishcloth

Instructions

Skill Level: Beginner

Size: 10 1/2 inches square

Materials: Lily Sugar'N Cream Cotton Yarn, or #4 Medium weight cotton yarn.

2 oz (56.7g) Approximately 95 yards

Tapestry or yarn needle

Needles: Size 9 (5.5mm) or size to obtain gauge.

Gauge: 4 sts and 6 rows = 1 inch

Cast on 43 sts.

Pattern

Row 1: K.

Row 2: Sl the first st. P across row.

Row 3: Sl the first st then K2tog across row.

Row 4: Sl the first st. *Make one, K1 rep from * across row.

> Make One: Make a new stitch by lifting the yarn in the space between the stitches. With the needle tip, lift the strand between the last stitch knit and the next stitch on the left hand needle and knit into the back of it. One knit stitch has been added.

Repeat rows 1-4 for pattern.

Repeat pattern rows until dishcloth measures 10 1/2 inches. Bind off.

Finishing

With tapestry or yarn needle weave in ends. Block if desired.

Sunshine Hanging Towel

Instructions

Skill Level: Easy

Size: 13 1/2 X 13 1/2 inches

Materials: Lily Sugar'N Cream Cotton Yarn, or and #4 Medium weight cotton yarn.

2.5 oz (70.9g) Approximately 120 yards

Tapestry or yarn needle

Sewing needle and matching thread

1- 1 inch button

Needles: Size 9 (5.5mm) or size to obtain gauge.

Gauge: 4 sts and 6 rows = 1 inch

Cast on 54 sts.

Pattern

Row 1: * P2, K1 rep from * across row.

Repeat row 1 until towel is 10 inches long.

Top Shaping

Row 1: (RS) *K1, K2tog, rep from * ending row with K2tog, K2. 36 sts.

Row 2: (WS) *K1, K2tog, rep from * to end of row. 24 sts.

Row 3: (RS) *K2tog across row. 12 sts.

Row 4-5: K across row.

Row 6: (WS) *K1, K2tog, rep from * to end of row. 8 sts.

Hanging Tab

Continue knitting each row on 8 sts until hanging tab measures 5 1/2 inches.

Buttonhole

Row 1: K2, K2tog, Yo twice, K2tog, K2.

Row 2: K3, K1 in first Yo, P1 in second Yo, K3.

Row 3-5: K across row.

Row 6: K2tog, K4, K2tog.

Row 7: Bind off.

Buttonhole Detail

Finishing

With tapestry needle, weave in ends. Sew button to the right side of the hanging towel as shown in photo.

Sunshine Dishcloth

Instructions

Skill Level: Beginner

Size: 10 1/2 inches square

Materials: Lily Sugar'N Cream Cotton Yarn, or #4 Medium weight cotton yarn.

2 oz (56.7g) Approximately 95 yards

Tapestry or yarn needle

Needles: Size 9 (5.5mm) or size to obtain gauge.

Gauge: 4 sts and 6 rows = 1 inch

Cast on 42 sts.

Pattern

Row 1: * P2, K1 rep from * across row.

Repeat row 1 until dishcloth is 10 1/2 inches long.

Bind off.

Finishing

With tapestry or yarn needle weave in ends. Block if desired.

Helpful Hints

Blocking

I may not always block a finished article I make for myself but I always block an item I will be giving as a gift. Blocking makes your stitches look nicer, smoothes edges, and ensures that it is the proper size and shape. Blocking is the use of water or steam to stretch and shape a finished piece. This process relaxes the stitches and settles them into shape. Blocking is especially important for natural fibers, however, man-made fibers also benefit from blocking. Knitted or crocheted laces almost always are blocked.

Blocking Tools

To begin blocking you will need a few things. You will need a flat, padded surface of a size that will support the entire piece that you will be blocking and pins. There are tools especially made for blocking which you may purchase on-line or at stores that sell fabrics or craft supplies.

Blocking Boards

Purchased blocking boards are made of heat-resistant materials and often have grids printed on them so you can easily measure your pieces. They can be pinned into and usually fold for storage. There are many ways to create your own blocking board or there are boards you can purchase at fabric or craft stores. The boards I prefer for blocking knitting and crochet projects are fabric cutting boards for large pieces and foam blocking board puzzle pieces for everything else.

Fabric Cutting Boards

Fabric cutting boards are great for larger projects. They are inexpensive, light weight, and store very easily. They fold into sections accordion style so they take up a minimal amount of storage space in your home. They are made of heavy-duty cardboard that is water resistant and have a white paper bonded to one side that is printed with color-fast measurement grids in both inches and centimeters. Opened to their full size most of them measure 40" wide x 72" long. Since pins are used to block with, keep in mind the surface underneath the board as you work. I pin into the board at an angle and the pin usually doesn't pierce the other side. You may also want to protect the surface underneath the board with a towel or blanket. You can use any of the three blocking methods for this board.

Foam Blocking Board Puzzle Pieces

These blocks are 12x12 inch squares that you snap together like a puzzle. Easy to use and compact, the blocks are inexpensive and can be arranged to fit long or irregularly shaped projects. You can create a long rectangle for scarves, a triangle for shawls or a square for sweaters.

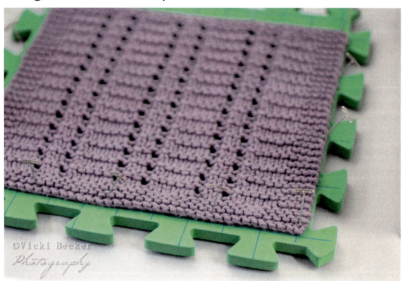

Pins

T-pins are often recommended for use when blocking knitting and crocheted pieces. They are like regular straight pins except the head is shaped like a T. They are easy to work with and are also rust-proof so you don't have to worry about leaving them in your piece while it dries.

Blocking Wires

For blocking lace and other large projects, you can purchase blocking wires, which are flexible metal wires that can help you block curves or the sides of a large project. The wires are woven in and out of the project and then reinforced with pins. The pins will keep the piece stretched to the correct dimensions on your board.

Blocking Methods

Wet blocking, spray blocking, and steam blocking are the three main methods of blocking a knitted or crocheted piece. The method used depends upon your personal preferences as well as the type of yarn used in the project. Wet blocking is an appropriate method for blocking man-made fibers and most natural fibers. Acrylic yarns are sensitive to heat and they should not be steam blocked. Always follow the care instructions on your yarn label when blocking.

Wet Blocking

Begin by washing your project according to yarn label instructions. Lay the piece flat on a clean towel and roll the towel, pressing out as much water as possible. Lay out your item on a flat, clean surface, such as a towel or blocking board, and pull it into the desired shape. Pin to a blocking board if desired. Let the piece air dry. As the piece dries, it will retain the shape that you gave it.

Spray Blocking

Spray blocking is the easiest and most gentle blocking process. All you need to do is lightly spray the finished piece with room-temperature water from a spray bottle. Get it damp enough to relax the fibers, but not soaking wet. Pull the item into the desired shape and pin in place. Let the piece air dry.

Steam Blocking

Steam blocking is a similar process to wet blocking except you use steam to relax the fibers instead of water. There are several different techniques when it comes to steam blocking. Some people stretch and pin their work to the desired shape before steaming, using the steam to help set the new shape. Others steam first and then pin, allowing the steam to relax the fibers. You can steam block with an iron or a hand-held steamer. The heat and moisture are the elements that are important, not the pressure of the iron. Never place an iron directly on a knitted or crocheted fabric. A pressing cloth is used between the iron and knitted or crocheted piece to protect. Hold the iron just above the fabric and let the steam dampen the piece completely. Then pin if necessary and leave to dry.

Conclusion

I hope you enjoyed the patterns. Please consider leaving me a review. I value your opinion and would love to hear from you.

You can also visit my facebook fan page to leave a message or comment.

http://www.facebook.com/VickiBeckerAuthor

Visit my author page at Amazon for a list of my other needlework titles!

http://www.amazon.com/-/e/B009ZWK7Q6

Visit my web site for more needlework tips and free patterns!

http://vickisdesigns.com

You can email me

vicki@vickisdesigns.com

Made in the USA
Middletown, DE
21 July 2025